The Width of Here

Silence is so accurate.

~ *Mark Rothko*

Also by L. Ward Abel

Peach Box and Verge (Little Poem Press)
Jonesing for Byzantium (UKA Press)
The Heat of Blooming (Pudding House Press)
Torn Sky Bleeding Blue (Erbacce Press)
Cousins Over Colder Fields (Finishing Line Press)
American Bruise (Parallel Press)
Roseorange (Flutter Press)
Little Town gods (Folded Word Press)
A Jerusalem of Ponds (Erbacce Press)
Digby Roundabout (Kelsay Books)
The Rainflock Sings Again (Unsolicited Press)
Floodlit (Beakful Press)

The WIDTH of Here

by

L. Ward Abel

720 – Sixth Street, Box # 5
New Westminster, BC
V3C 3C5   CANADA

Title: The Width of Here
Author: L. Ward Abel
Cover Photo: by L. Ward Abel
Layout and Cover Design: Candice James
Editor: Candice James

All rights reserved including the right to reproduce or translate this book or any portions thereof, in any form without the permission of the publisher. Except for the use of short passages for review purposes, no part of this book may be reproduced, in part or in whole, or transmitted in any form or by any means, electronically or mechanically, including photocopying, recording, or any information or storage retrieval system without prior permission in writing from the publisher or a licence from the Canadian Copyright Collective Agency (Access Copyright).

www.silverbowpublishing.com
info@silverbowpublishing.com
ISBN: 9781774031490 print book
ISBN: 9781774031506 e book
© Silver Bow Publishing 2021

Library and Archives Canada Cataloguing in Publication

Title: The width of here / by L. Ward Abel.
Names: Abel, L. Ward, author.
Description: Poems.
Identifiers: Canadiana (print) 20210103523 | Canadiana (ebook) 2021010354X | ISBN 9781774031490
   (softcover) | ISBN 9781774031506 (HTML)
Classification: LCC PS3601.B45 W53 2021 | DDC 811/.6—dc23

Acknowledgements:

"Your Breathing"—*Honest Ulsterman*
"Pilgrim"—*The Charleston Anvil*
"Eyes Fixed on the Painter"—*Bosque*
"All of Our Living—*Ariel Chart*
"All Shadows Point North"—*The Arkansan Review*
"Breakfast"—*Deep South Magazine*
"Keats on a Train"—*Whistling Shade*
"Unanimity" and "Holding Years"—*Concrete Desert Review*
"These Winter Fields"—*Worcester Review*
"Civilization"—*Nixes Mate Review*
"The Quiet Days"—*Flare Journal*
"I Begin to Sense the Burning of Books" —*The Wild Word*
"The Ground Gives Way—*The Wild Word*
"Down to the shell of what was a store"—*The Phare*
"Miller's Thumb"—*Rattle*
"Wide as the Summer Dusk"—*Grand Little Things*
"The Ease of Being"—*Macrina Magazine*
"Conversation with Rothko"—*Curiouser Magazine*
"Between Butler and Columbus" —*The Electric Rail*
"Crow Song" —*The Electric Rail*

The Width of Here

TABLE OF CONTENTS:

Coming to Ground ... 11
Your Breathing ... 12
Glory ... 13
Keats on a Train ... 14
Pilgrim ... 15
Eyes Fixed on the Painter ... 16
Breakfast ... 17
Breaks ... 18
Longer Days from Now to June ... 19
These Winter Fields ... 20
All Shadows Point North ... 21
Unanimity ... 22
Numbers ... 23
Holding Years ... 24
All Our Living ... 25
Night Releases the Ink ... 26
Old Clothes ... 27
Dignity ... 28
The Approach ... 29
Rio Paz ... 31
Storm Outside ... 33
Boundary Trees ... 34
Civilization ... 35
The Quiet Days ... 36
I Begin to Sense the Burning of Books ... 37
The Ground Gives Way ... 38
My Anxious Dinner ... 39
War ... 40
Friction ... 41
Crow Song ... 42
Down to the Shell of What Was a Store ... 44
Miller's Thumb ... 45
A Clearing ... 46

The Width of Here

The Heavy Countryside Exhausted ... 47
Closure ... 48
Between Butler and Columbus ... 49
Land ... 50
Wide as the Summer Dusk ... 51
Comfort ... 52
Free Will and Geology ... 53
Light ... 54
Sequence ... 55
Halo ... 56
The Ease of Being ... 57
Portion ... 58
The Blue Dragonfly ... 59
Between Mind and Memory ... 60
Fields of Scree ... 61
Do the Blind Circles ... 62
Conversation with Rothko ... 63

Author's Bio ... 65

O the mind, mind has mountains, cliffs of fall
Frightful, sheer, no-man-fathomed.

~ *Gerard Manley Hopkins*

The Width of Here

Coming to Ground

Sear blows over
like yellow butterflies.
Souls are in the grove.

Trees rattle an end
that rises, dims
like breathing,
moves through
like moving
and gone.

Sure enough
the angling of light
looks even later.

Hear the sound
limbs make when
they come to ground.

Your Breathing

Here,
      leaning-in
           to get a better view
    I think while sunning
        full faced
    there's poignance in my brevity.

        Truth shows up.

The metal's edge
    makes a cicatrice
        of a once-clean place.

Geography rises
    then breathes out.

Perfume on my hands,
    Arabian,
can't distract from the tattoo
    that is my room.

        I join your breathing.
        It teems.
        It crowds.

Glory

Hear the rattle
        in the grove again
a gesture followed by birds' returning
        even as they slope
               away and back
        through broken clouds.

        Sundown waters a sea
              300 miles
                  south.

How poignant
        receiving your Christmas card
after you'd gone on to Glory,
        with my own birthday
               coming the next month.

        And woods will complete
               the ring.

Keats on a Train

I saw Keats on the train today.
      He looked speechless,
           but I was speechless too.

      Help me, Keats, I thought,
          tell me about survival,
              about living.

Surely, you would know.
      I almost asked out loud
          but didn't, couldn't
  on this Thursday
 an almost-day, a gray day,
and a silent one.

Later I wrote down questions for him,
     respectful of his decease.

          Where are you now?
     Did you go home?
Is it beautiful there?
    Is it true there?
        Do words really matter?
  Do you live with God?

        Do words really matter?
        Do words really matter?
        Does anything matter?

If I see him again,
    I'll give him the questions.
But I may have missed my chance.

Pilgrim

I'm alone
though the world is here.
I choose this moment
and this one to hold,
and it all feels poignant and right
in its wrongness.

    My spleen shows its age,
    takes the form of thunder
    from rained-out skies ...
    but rain is coming again.

Like everything alive
I look for exits when entering,
am double-edged
depending on the light.

    I have a pocket Wordsworth
    and other bibles packed
    in case of breaking camp.
    I'm on ready.

        My noisy head
        is night-loud on a river porch
        like childhood,
        but I've had faith enough for abiding
        sometimes in the nearly dark
        between great gathered trees
        where red storms pop above,
        go to pulse, then are quiet.

But whether through bunting
of a low black ceiling
or a day's new tinge—
the river
is the same.

Eyes Fixed on the Painter

Already four o'clock
                and the day's been thieved again
        into showers, into sheets,
    a long time coming.

        I'm a million self-portraits
      eyes fixed on the painter,
          distracted, marking time
                in late afternoon rains.

          This life has an edge;
      its living conjures death,
    replicating, crowding out
what it brings and dispatches.

Breakfast

Morning dims, brightens,
        rain starts to pond at the mountain's base.
Sunday the green, these creases
        divide our great sloping continent
            into chutes, they spill directions
                named by us
            but the compass doesn't care.

        Limits, edges, endings, starts
            mirror and fail to tell a seed from fallen timber,
                run through my thoughts,
        hover, land, dissipate,
return to leaving,
        all in the name of steam.

Where the knelling stops
        south of roses,
    north of stones,
        I find comfort in my breakfast
            and its lack of a seam
        with the full-blown night.

Breaks

You'll notice the gap in my journal.
It approaches six weeks, even longer.
You'll wonder why the writing basically
stopped, scattered, awoke in time for later.
There may be other questions, questions about
shadows and space and curtains that didn't move
even with windows cracked or opened. Later you
will disregard the gap altogether and return
to your life, to your own moments of darkness and light.
But the break in my journal will still be here, still with an
open quiet mouth.

Longer Days from Now to June

Longer days from now to June
when fields erupt in solstice.

Today begins inching sunlight
longer every morning.

        The rains fill aquifers
        a hundred miles south of here
        and spring up from the ridgeline,
        as a shadow of shorter night
        shudders in the starting-up.

And all in search of a bloom.

These Winter Fields

A dank passage cuts through
to a cedared gate
and I'm in the winter fields.

No blue, like blue above,
where foothills stand up
against much older seas,
only beaches left behind
in a gathering of sand
and greenery south of here.

The brevity of change
that never ends, it shows
in the crows too,
 perched on the branches
of my lungs. And if all of this
were to become unfamiliar,
no landmarks to get me home,
just folds where
other people's houses
dot the weal,
I'd shelter in place.

It's a red cedar gate, I think,
small knives that belie
their being green.

All Shadows Point North

I've got a clear view of the west here,
        losing interest in eastern drones
              up and down the coast.

Dryer air,
        the air of jaggedness—

            October always scares me.
    Its lines too clean:
bolded black edges,
        mortality, all waking thoughts, the moment.

Like coyotes, the world rummages
        through my garbage.

Across the creek bottom, into woods,
        I rummage too.

            As the flyway moans
        due east of me I hear the train
on its way to Manchester.
        It drops down to farmlands
            through feathers
and the brass of autumn.

I melt back along the creek beds
        and find convergence,
            hearing my name
                spoken like it's misspelled,
            sung like a crow sings.

            The air shifts to a southerly.
            All shadows point north.

Unanimity

Redwings pour out
from any number of trees
      a formation, a singularity
      then a sky.

They crowd the edges,
    a few drops
        but holding,
           brimming
        not straying away from
    the local common lung,
and comforted in their unanimity
      like a thermal black flag
        c a s t
      into weather.

Numbers

Part of the flood, it brims
and I am one of many.

Clouds' juice
just an aggregate,
a cottony lake up there.

Each pixel represents a soul.

Then I join the rain.
        I am become ...
                water.

Holding Years

What to figure
when another one is gone?

        I won't live along
        Headstone Road
        with no way to cross over.

        I'll stay close to the source
        of all words and soul.

After all a million multiverses
    only spark a little bit
        then a flicker across
            a square, dark, lonely space.

            A vine-covered place
        that can't go back
and can't outlive itself.

Like dragonflies
    the nations, woods,
        patterns, flocks,
           beteemed
    chains of followers
speckled with leaders,

        they lead to shallows
        where *now* is replaced
        with another *now*—
        and all tumble through
        taking-in almost nothing.

    But my gathering
    can't be held
    or even weighed.

All Our Living

There's a jumping
       between trees
                      a slight elevation
              luring wings
                      across,
                      along,
                      among.

       A refusal to cede,
       a greening back to gray
       becomes part of me.

Catching my breath
just after pneumonia,
            I glide.
            I see the air.

The sky holds
      all of our living,
           holds me and my chatter,
                    holds you.

Night Releases the Ink

Night releases the ink
with stars—
with evening stars
and a small moon.

Each has a pulse
through barbasol breaks
above.

Sounding like Piazzolla
a few birds ride along the path
and away.

The amber line is gone;
it's a city in the west now
losing light, relenting finally
to the much stronger night.

Old Clothes

I live in woods
        like old clothes
                draped over rocks
                        the size of towns
                sky-facing, totemic
    some worn away by water.

The angle falls
        like fall-line slate.
                It gives into sand
                still two-hundred miles
                        up from the gulf.

There my tunneled flesh
        occurs to me
                as being mostly mind
                        but less a knowing—
        the con-job of thought
plus breathing.

    Too full of soul
            for a house of flint.
                      my dreams spill into sunrise—
        dreams like rain on dry ground
    form a wash kin to dying.

A rivulet presumes.
                Then the piedmont sweats.

    I churn,
        I wear the water,
                      the woods,
            the stone.

        A ritual.

Dignity

Ask, in every move
and flinch, every act,
if there's a purpose to
what good you've done.

And like the confluence of all
rivers draining all continents
and skies, know there's dignity
in the fall.

The Approach

A profile of trees
hugs the high places
above.

I can see through
        to gray, blue
                at an angle;
      bristles stand over
               a steep drop-off

                      d
                      o
                      w
                      n

                below.

The ground rises
to meet the lowering
and, in between,
water runs all
              o
          r   u
      a   n
         d

        like patience.

Light comes, goes,
        never stays but
                is never far from staying.

                    Hills and gaps
            and valleys
                exhale
            in wide open country.

The Width of Here

There are places elsewhere
       with no shoulder-room,
                       just people,
                     steam.

But here
       the vista shows
             a topsoil curve—
      its vanishing point,
its crease.

             The flaws.

Rio Paz

In the courtyard by the river
    rain drips from awning
        furled like a canopy
            of aluminum and green sugar.

    Lorca's book of poetry
        sweats letters on a wicker chair.
    He was buried in an unmarked grave,
            they say.

Would-be hawks and trucks
    compete in town,
        a smattering of flashes and pops—
            they could be an awakening.

            But thinkers get distracted.
            Questions forget.

        A bold day of reflection
    should find a garden,
all tools replaced with pens.

    But see the scops navigate traffic,
        dumb-asses, self-pointed,
            while the beautiful city falls.

They give names to small streams
    like hurricane names,
        but still the streams are small.

The dying breed—with dying art
from more than a keyboard,
        a parcel of conflict in and out of meaning
        knotted like fishing nets and word fronds
            and the remains of fiddler crabs—
                should now compose.

The Width of Here

Exhume that patch you're standing on—
    otherwise the first casualty
        could be the past
            because just under the peel
    is something gone the way of breath.

        So hide your sentences
        in small corners
        creases, gaps, wicker,
        carefully folded, considered
        in a quiet place alone, free.
        Always free.

We walk on porous   ground.
    It holds no water
           but has a current of souls.

Sometimes when ferries
    are closed upriver,
        folks get stranded on the banks.

            But others transfigure
            out to sea, silent,
            leaving only

        charaCters.

Storm Outside

The sun always shines in here
but a storm outside marks the time.

        God bless our supply chains
        even as jazz plays Bags and Trane
        and my books can't be taken away.

    Anything that moves proves the universe.

  I take and eat in the vestibule—
        still
  a storm outside marks the time.

The Width of Here

Boundary Trees

A few minutes before the weather hits
    I hear a growl, a tone under the ear,
        more feel than actual note;
            it rattles and shows
        like a thousand firework bursts
    coming from behind the curtain
and it moves this way.

    The clay and light conduct,
        combine into a swimmer's road.

            The wind self-fulfills, touches,
        becomes more senses than we are.

In a voice like Lincoln's but deep as a god's
    it lays low the boundary trees;
        their purpose, submission, asunder
like something that burns.

        Division becomes academic.

        The house has no center,
    no low place for us to stow away.

And it roars up the angled weal
    like angry kettle drums …

        like Bosnia in the nineties.

Civilization

Winds blow the timbers
holding up the porch.
    I hear thunder to the north,
    making strange the evening voice,
    second day of spring.

    The sun tilts; it still burns
    like Sherman's Columbia,
conjures shadows
into lengths of prophecy,
    eventually stretching to combine
    into a night we don't recognize.

        Aroused by southerlies
        the blooming starts; it spreads
        across my flashing countryside.

The Quiet Days

The black-line edge
           along canopies of various green
      interrupts, blends,
           but is other than the sky.

Availability of light
      determines truth, which explains
why dread of twilight and dark
      drapes everything above ground.

                      The mind-sized universe
                      strains at the now
                      whose borders blur
                      like late day film.

            The highest part
            of the afternoon dome
            flickers a spotted view.

A waterfall of blue
belies magma below
parceled into farms
with shoes to match our
burning: tightened, distancing
            almost overlapping,
            more huddled than before.

      All this must be a song I dreamed,
            one played by a brass band at sundown
      long after the gig has ended.

            There under velvet stars
      I see for miles the rows of radio towers
            just starting their broadcast night.

I Begin to Sense the Burning of Books

I begin to sense the burning of books.
Opposition has become criminalized. The other.
They are unworthy of opinion. I wonder how it came to this.

I begin to sense few to no places of refuge,
even looking at various satellite images from above.
Fair is foul sure enough without a way to leave.

I hear a piano painting with large and small brushes—
it drapes the block, the grid, appealing and appalling.
The tedium of chaos answers yes.

I begin to sense the end of something.
It's cheap to mention Constantinople but, damn,
tell the monks to record us using paper made of water.

The Ground Gives Way

In high mountain air
lightning from counties
fifty miles behind a series of ridges
flashes quiet, slow
like bubbles, enlightenment,
epiphanic at various locations
along the spine of Atlas.

My God the sounds in the night
and so many in succession,
the world, the storm,
we watch news like fireworks, like Dresden,
the view made counter-intuitive
      love thy neighbor
except in righteous acts of vengeance.

Sometimes the ground gives way
so full of rain as to confuse
earth with sky and lose balance
at elevations above and beyond
the mortar, glue of our tongue-
in-groove granite
temples.

My Anxious Dinner

Plates clatter
    late afternoon.

Prodigal dragons in flight
    outside on the short lawn.

        In authentic present tense I cower.

    The land is a stew
made of green bell-curve peppers
    a harvest from rocky
        blood-red, blue-ridge fields.

    I won't forgive the chef
for bringing me
    the good and broken
        all at once—making true
            my anxious dinner.

War

I.

Shale ceiling
granite roof,
floors made of water,
windows—paper hats,
doors are suggestions.

II.

Piano fills the vacuum
like Bartók. The player
vows incessance until
the war is over.
Prolific composer.

III.

Outside, there being
no substitute for rain,
the green washes red
from the land.
Ancestors huddle.

Friction

Hitched to a losing proposition
        all dissonance
               drops choreography.

Once there were planets,
      like crows,
           they circled a greater sun,
                but nobody recalls
           the sting of chaos or anxiety
      that first incentivized order.

                Now high-plains grass stands
        as the only friction
    between disarray and us.

Crow Song

A glass door opens
and scares four or five like him,
swarms that had been a pack.

While others re-form
one flies alone slowly
along those night-green walls.

In the road round a corner
he scatters to and from a smear
waiting to bake.

He has doll eyes.
They blink a language—
utterly means to an end.

A glare formed,
reforming, reactive.

On watch and not.
Life in the wake of cars.

Near the graveyard
he competes with yellow butterflies;
they dance, endorse, convoy down
the country's summer-fade,
call, respond
all near an old primitive church.

Pines and green canal rights-of-way
roll down from there
to where he'll cross over those rows.

Sometimes he and the blues
will fuss, go silent, fuss again;
then conjure burning fields,

divide the world into parcels
of blackwing clash
and long-frayed oaths,
while the Irish harp
or the other one
wails a river bottom gale,
a crow song, a waterspout—
swollen little hurricane.

No wonder he mistakes sunrise for sunset,
huddles on skeleton oaks ragged with ivy.
But he'll catch the first and last
from up there—
his feathers, like film,
will peel the layers
show the daylight.

All we ever have.

Down to the Shell of What Was a Store

Down to the shell
of what was a store's four corners
      concrete block vines climb the wet walls
           and no roof blocks out the sky
                from all that comes with it.

    It's years later
since heart first went-the-knuckle with time.

      Today even ghosts have abandoned such places.

         The world's not the same world.
         The song's not the same song.

So much has gone from here
      only to be replaced with whirrs, flashes, clangs.

Out back on an old metal sign,
    an unrecognizable face
        rusted and nailed to a post,
           strains to send a message out
    to anyone who'll listen.

His cries oxidize when hitting the air
    like the way of the holy,
        whose example can only be, at most,
    pencil-shading a blank sheet
        to find shadow words.

But there is salvation in damaged goods
    and no growth in perfection.

        At solstice and equinox
      the rising sun comes straight through
      where a door used to latch.

Miller's Thumb

I.

How deep is the green skin
        out to the east and away
                into wideness?

        Aerial shots taken without consent
                show just how alone we are.

And nobody said anything
        about consequences.
                So, no escape this time.

        We're known by our remaining,
not how we arrive.

II.

Pages don't turn;
they're burned.

        Be careful
        what you fish for.
                You could kill it.
                And poets are the first to go.

        Riddle me the weight of civilization.

                But scales vary
                with the miller's thumb.

A Clearing

I've got a clearing now
      carved in from the tree line.
            Its hollow
bends away from open field.

In the center of it
      crags a bloom of dogwood;
            behind are darker waves
of young, thin poplar
      under oak.

            The world has changed again.

Those shocks, shudders
      belie a perfect quiet spring
            scoping
      across, above,
            east to west.

My clearing has a brick-high boundary
      along a slight
            where barbed fence
used to mark two pastures.

I have become insensitive to edges,
      their scars are numb as old maps.

The Heavy Countryside Exhausted

The sky is gray bubble-wrap
        creek voices crossing bottom land.
            Then shifts a wind
                  away to quiet.

        It droops the heavy countryside exhausted.

            You should never take direction
            from the sound a shadow makes.

Closure

Great they fall
and not even tears.

A bloom acts as bowl
catches what passes for grief
in our common loss.

        An old woman wails,
        so the story starts,
        like revolution
        isn't always a good thing.

But rained-out
powder blue ceilings
never break through
and powder blue eyes
never find closure.

        Still you know
        skies at night
        are never quite empty.

Between Butler and Columbus

Late. Red.
Thunderhead-soaked sundown
almost a whole county wide
in an otherwise
purple clarity.

Not from radar but conveyed
through dead-reckoning
and Kentucky windage,
a blood-colored marble range,
its innards flashing pregnant.

Due south,
its base hidden by the curve,
is the great churn
with outer walls of veined lightning
a full eighty miles away.

Land

Shorn,
we grow among our fallen.

    Exposed,
        the war waits for rain
            impatient for peace—
        ragged,
        resurrecting in loops.

        The pasturage drones
      in a voice strained by experience—
            calls us
              to never burn our homes again
        because ghosts tend to rise
            from the dark.

    Just before half-light
        it begins to mist—
            first like whispers in a prison yard
            a holy spring—
                then grace.

Wide as the Summer Dusk

A blur of worlds
      at elevations
           where heaven starts,
    indistinguishing space, clouds, rain
and the very tops,
    land and tree,
        all in this blue air.

Places with views of the weather
clear the deck of distraction;
like the false security of radar,
         seeing-is-confirming,
    looking for probabilities
where no certainties survive the winter.

Steering wheel
wide as a summer dusk,
      the farther back I stand
         the more the circles merge
            and all direction erased.

        As the sun rises
        it sets somewhere
        in a tandem dance.

Bells chime
      as the curtain comes down the gap
        and across lesser hills to where I am,
    flummoxed into believing
        change is almost always good.

Comfort

Birds have flocked like jazz
        on my water oak
               with voices
                      just above the low rumbled log-rolling
        west east of summer varieties.

Reminds of guns of gods
        getting closer, artillery, convulsed.
                Like Stalingrad making small circles
                      over and over.

        Like the constant dragonflies—
                on perpetual missions.
        Their thunder can rip your head off
                take your home.

It tried to rainbow today.
        Colors bled out,
                the sun looked away.
                      I crossed the field
                to see a cloud collapse on itself,
                      and I've seen no deer lately.

A persimmon tree,
        like a lightning rod,
                surveils my dragon-flight.
        To lose myself on a few lawns.
                For a short time.
        Then fly apart.

Life has a sharp blade.
                Don't come here
                for comfort, please,
                my noisy head.

                      Please.

Free Will and Geology

"A fair price for consciousness"
                      ~ Galway Kinnell

The great souls concluded long ago
that being is a choice.

A mind can break like pine
from the sound of short-lived breathing
or, more than just mass and motion,
it can be the face looking up through dark
to see the colored glass of silence
and the light behind the panes.

                God sings a frozen note
            over streets, fields, rivers
                    and down
              to make the sacred tides.

Damned repellant
geology of night,
dread, anger and loss—

            I aspire to waters
       while flying inside intinctions
              of the sunlit rain.

Light

    has been explained to me
             as the opposite of a total lack,
                       and being void of night.

                    All senses combined
                      are just a ripple to kingdom come,
       and scatter rhymes with matter
                for a reason.

Holy photons
        bathe the gathered.

                    They—
              the body of God
                  the harvest
           of pillowed scythes.

Sequence

    I.

A flourish from running doves
just airborne off a gutter
catches my quiet
by surprise.

        II.

    Almost transparent wings
    defy the ground's appeal
    unaccustomed to such density
    and airspace being wide.

            III.

        Notice that the sound of wind
        from former leaves
        on former trees
        can still be heard
        in these long-cleared fields.

Halo

This butterfly
      in a moment of showers,
           a devil-beats-his-wife,
              seeks the magnolia sheen,
    a siren, a bloom
like a lighthouse.

                She treads the smaller thermals,
                   part of a halo
                      encircling all trees.

Le Papillon,
      she dries what beads remain
           with brightness,
                a self-made fan.

           But then again, her torn sky
      bleeding blue into fields,
a bruise the size of weather sheet-flows,
      and she finds shelter,
           overgrown, there—
yellow, black, wet
                at rest.

The Ease of Being

To have a view of the sky
        this year of all years
               in the eye of a played-out hurricane.

With the ease of being,
      the wind now goes another way.

To have an ear that's open
        and anger porous as a hedge,
            impervious to sea water
                but no match for truth
           when slow to gnash.

      Colors harden with time;
           what are jagged were soft and green,
               their edges blurred.

        Somewhere
the rain's as thin as blue sky ...

        But not here.

Portion

Just like a Jain,
    I'm careful to step
        where nothing else is,
    and when I feel something
        under my foot
  I lean away
      I try, while going.

My portion parades
    like screenplay up to now
        and now and again
            I relate it all to sparrows;
        they fly near the eyes
    of my passing through.

The Blue Dragonfly

At the end of beginning to end,
                            he levitates.

Late in the season between radar red scatterings
                        there's a dronish air to his honor.

        He gets in the door before I can shut it.

                While in a new cosm—controlled, unfree
        he freezes, things now a matter of license,
or life, more to the point.

He need not have questioned my empathy
                as my hands urge the way to Glory,
      out over across his unkempt
                          width of here.

Between Mind and Memory

A shadow crosses the lawn,
       lit from above,
              a shape cast in green with wings.

              What a view I have,
         knowing places look different
      depending on whether I'm arriving
or going away.

The gap between mind and memory
      is where everything lives,
not just scrolling through a line,
              a finger-touch,
              a screen,
              a point.

        It takes the form
        of all we're among,
          made of inches, miles, time.

But I've already left,
mid-flight
between the yard
and the nearest star.

Fields of Scree

They still find bodies along old trails here
        in fields of scree when the snow has melted
                and the air's gone dry.

On a night like tonight
        when dew is only cool to the touch,
                souls have been known to ghost
                        and be mistaken for steam.

                But steam can't
        follow these faulted, crossing tracks.

                        No.

                They are the breeze
        of those much better than ourselves.

Do the Blind Circles

Bats—
        before
                the powder-blue-to-red
        western sky of former suns
can retreat—
        do the blind circles
                paper-thick
                through amber lines of night
        and orbit in all directions
                from east
to the left of north.

Conversation with Rothko

Red

The world is not a kind world.
It's best to realize this.

Red doesn't occur in nature;
we seek it through our fear of red.

Colors are ghosts of bone-houses
gone now to seed.

Blue

The opposite of windows
is the open air.

Darkness in the foreground
brings alive the western skies.

And wind can give texture to things
that cannot, will not move.

Green

I had wished to hold a moment,
an aerial view of the counties.

Death is peace, water flows
uphill and clocks aren't veined.

We can count to nothing and start again,
or else become the leaves that we are.

Black

A magnet for vision draws-in all eyes
and itself and sings.

One is one is none is everything but
even light can't escape.

Unsex the sunset,
take it to the perfect night of prayer.

White

Painters have nothing to say anymore,
they flood the intersection with bright

bright light, play God,
make holy the vacant.

I walk out of the chapel
into a glaring absence.

Yellow

There is no yellow in point of fact; it's only
suggested by an empty width out before us.

Don't offer heat to the cold morning,
add nothing, remain, stop your painting.

But we aren't at home here.
Otherwise we would just breathe.

Author Profile

L. Ward Abel is a poet, composer, spoken-word performer, teacher, and retired lawyer. He has been published hundreds of times in print and online worldwide, and is the author of two full collections and ten chapbooks of poetry. He has also written and recorded twelve albums of music to date under the pseudonym Max Able, with the group Abel & Rawls, and with Abel, Rawls and Hayes, along with being a founding member of Atlanta spoken-word pioneers Scapeweavel. Abel resides in rural Georgia.

The Width of Here

www.ingramcontent.com/pod-product-compliance
Lightning Source LLC
Chambersburg PA
CBHW070050120526
44589CB00034B/1874